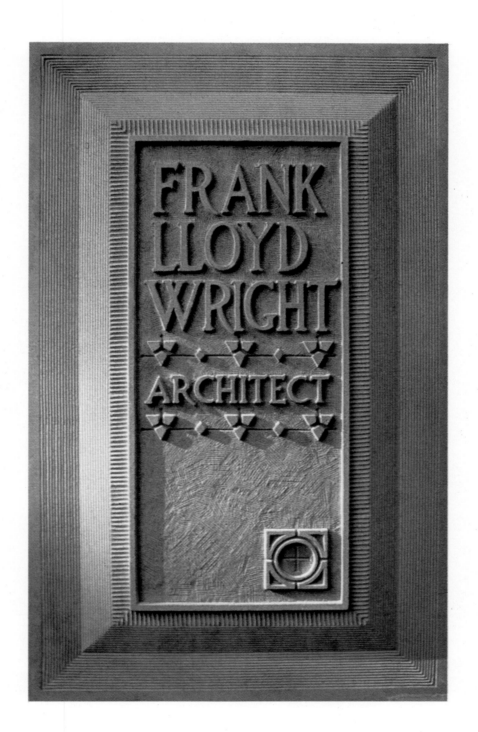

Frank Lloyd Wright

Maria Costantino

Crescent Books
New York/Avenel, New Jersey

This 1991 edition published by Crescent Books,
distributed by Outlet Book Company, Inc.,
a Random House Company,
40 Engelhard Avenue
Avenel, New Jersey 07001

Produced by
Brompton Books Corporation
15 Sherwood Place
Greenwich, CT 06830

ISBN 0-517-05291-1

8 7 6 5 4 3 2

Printed in Hong Kong

Page 1:
Outside wall plaque from the
Frank Lloyd Wright House and
Studio, Oak Park, IL

Page 2:
Robie House, Chicago, 1909.

Pages 4-5
Meyer May House, Grand
Rapids, Michigan, 1909. Rear
extension built 1920.

Contents

Introduction   6

Early Works   20

The Prairie House   38

Influences and
New Materials   54

New Ideas and the
Usonian House   66

The Next One   88

Index   112

INTRODUCTION

On June 8th 1869 in Richland Center, Wisconsin, Frank Lloyd Wright, the greatest American architect of the twentieth century, was born. Wright's father, William Russell Cary Wright, came from an English family of non-conformists who had emigrated and settled in New England. After leaving Amherst College, where he had studied law, William Wright made his living as a traveling music teacher in the Mid-West of America, and in Wisconsin he met and married his first wife, Permilia Holcomb, by whom he had three children. On his wife's death in 1864, William Wright resumed his wanderings, apparently abandoning his children.

Not long after this he met Anna Lloyd-Jones at a music festival, and despite the difference in their ages – he was 46, she was 29 – they fell in love and were soon married. While her husband was passionate about music, Anna Wright had a deep respect for education, something that was to affect and influence her son's whole life.

In 1874 William Wright took his new family back to his native New England, to Weymouth, Massachusetts, then a rural village not far from Boston. Here William Wright was parson at Weymouth's small Baptist Church. Two years later the family traveled to Philadelphia to visit the great Centennial Exhibition. It was here that Anna Wright was to discover the Froebel kindergarten concept, a radical departure from infant teaching approaches. It seems that Anna Wright had already decided that her son Frank was destined to become an architect and she realized just how beneficial this type of education would be for him. On returning to Massachusetts, Anna Wright made enquiries in Boston and discovered that one of Froebel's students, Mrs Kraus-Boelte, had opened a kindergarten in the city in 1872. Since it was impossible for Frank to travel each day to kindergarten in Boston, Anna bought all the necessary equipment and started Frank's lessons at home.

At seven years old, Frank was well beyond kindergarten age, yet Anna Wright remained determined. The Froebel approach to kindergarten teaching encouraged children to play; without their realizing it, their play was transformed into a recognition and appreciation of natural objects and the basic laws on which adult life depends. Children were offered toys as 'gifts,' but the toys were not pretty things like dolls, but simply shaped objects in primary colors. Initially, the toys or gifts were limited to three basic shapes: the cube, the cylinder, and the sphere, with which dozens of games could and would be played, and which gradually progressed in difficulty. Starting by arranging the two-dimensional shapes into patterns, the children advanced to three-demensional structures and were encouraged to call on their imaginative skills to name their final structures – a boat, a house, or whatever they had envisaged.

By this method children were gradually instructed that these simple geometric forms were the basis of all natural appearances, and for Frank Lloyd Wright the two- and three-dimensional Froebelian schemes and exercises were to exert a long-lasting influence on his approach to architecture, with his emphasis on the direct expression of function and simple forms.

Some time around 1880 the Wright family, by this time including two daughters, Jane and Maginel, were back in Wisconsin, this time in the state capital, Madison, where the family occupied a wooden cottage in Gorham Street. During their vacations from the Second Ward School, the Wright children lived and worked on the Lloyd-Jones farm at Spring Green. The periods spent on the farm not only familiarized the young Wright with physical labor, but brought him closer to his mother's relatives and their love of the land.

Back in Madison, however, there was a constantly widening breach between his parents, and in 1885 William Wright deserted his family, never to return. At around sixteen years of age, Frank Lloyd Wright found himself at the head of the family with the additional problem of supporting it financially.

Almost immediately, Anna Wright launched her son's career: in the Madison directory of 1885 an entry listed reads 'Frank L Wright, draftsman' and her son was placed in the office of a local builder, Allen D Connover, not as a draftsman, however, but as an office boy and most junior apprentice.

Connover was the sole professional builder in Madison at this time; he was not essentially an architect, since his bias was towards engineering and not design. In addition to supervising the construction of buildings designed by others, Connover was also the Dean of Engineering at the University. Consequently, what Wright learnt in Connover's office were lessons in engineering practice and the sorts of jobs he was required to undertake were more than just paperwork. In his autobiography, Wright describes a typical task of installing metal clips on the roof trusses of the Science Hall building at the University during the winter of its construction. For the two years that Wright was in Connover's employ, he was allowed time off each day to take courses in the Department of Engineering under the Dean, his boss, and one Professor Bull. It was as

Right: Frank Lloyd Wright and his family assembled on the steps of his Oak Park home. They are, from left, Uncle Jenkin Lloyd Jones, Aunt Susan, sister Jane, wife Catherine holding son Lloyd, mother Anna Lloyd Wright, sister Maginel, Frank Lloyd Wright and cousin Mary.

close as Wright would ever get to an architectural training. Of the four-year course comprising of technical instruction and practice in drafting, Wright's total academic attendance was less than two years, for in the early summer of 1887, Frank Lloyd Wright ran off to Chicago.

Wright's departure for Chicago has often been viewed as a calculated risk: his lack of formal training or higher education was balanced by his skills and knowledge of good construction learnt in Connover's office and all the aesthetic theories he had learnt from reading the works of John Ruskin. Finding employment was made somewhat easier, however, by his introduction to Joseph Lyman Silsbee, an easterner by birth and a practitioner of East-Coast-style architecture, derived in part from the works of Norman Shaw and his English contemporaries.

By 1887 Silsbee had become a much-sought-after designer of simple yet elegant 'Shingle Style' houses. Furthermore, Silsbee had also been commissioned by Reverend Jenkin Lloyd-Jones, Wright's uncle, to design a new building for All Souls' Church, whose congregation had outgrown its meeting place in a store in Cottage Grove Avenue. Wright, it appears, had learnt about this commission before he left Wisconsin and, so the legend goes, with the last four dollars in his pocket, he was introduced to Silsbee and was set to work the next day on the All Souls'

project. The design was peculiar for a church as Silsbee's style was strongly domestic. The church resembled more a suburban home or clubhouse with its informal, assymetrical design and mix of brickwork and brown shingles.

Wright's formal employment in Silsbee's office, however, was to last only seven or eight months, up until the fall of 1887 when he joined the offices of Adler and Sullivan. It seems that Wright was growing increasingly restless and was eager to move on to new challenges. But he never quite forgot Silsbee nor the lessons he had learnt, for in his early works in the 1890s and later in the 1940s, the basis of much of Wright's work was his tendency to incorporate polygonal elements into the plans of his buildings, elements that can be traced back to Silsbee.

Hearing of a vacancy at the offices of Adler and Sullivan in the fall of 1887, Wright applied for the position of draftsman. For several nights prior to the interview, Wright stayed up late in order to prepare a selection of drawings to show Sullivan. Some of the drawings were reworkings of Silsbee's drawings and designs for ornaments, while others were deliberately 'Sullivanesque.' During the interview Sullivan studied the drawings and Wright was hired at 25 dollars a week.

Boston-born Louis Sullivan (1856-1924) lived for most of his childhood with his grandparents who encouraged him in his studies and love of nature. By the age of sixteen, Sullivan knew he wanted to be an architect and at seventeen he enrolled at the Massachusetts Institute of Technology. His student days were, however, shortlived, and Sullivan left M I T a year later to work in Philadelphia with Frank Furness (1839-1912), an architect of somewhat eccentric buildings, and then in Chicago with William Le Baron Jenney (1832-1907), one of the first architects of steel-framed buildings. Nine months later, Sullivan returned to academic training in Paris at the École des Beaux-Arts. Unsuited to formal education, Sullivan once more abandoned his studies in favor of visiting Rome and looking at the works of Michelangelo.

On his return to the United States, Sullivan settled in Chicago and established a partnership with Dankmar Adler (1844-1900) who was largely responsible for handling the business and technical aspects of the practice.

In addition to designing buildings, Sullivan also wrote about his approaches to architecture and he stated his belief that old styles, traditions, and values, both in architecture and in society, had little place in the new modern America. Sullivan also believed that the finest source of inspiration was nature itself. Most of Sullivan's buildings in the 1880s, however, were not the 'expansive' and 'rhythmic growths' that he desired, but still variations of ideas by Furness and Henry Hobson Richardson (1838-86), one of America's most progressive architects.

When Wright joined the firm of Adler and Sullivan, the practice and Sullivan were on the threshold of a brilliant career having just been awarded the widely coveted commission for the design of the Auditorium Building in Chicago. The building was complex in both its planning and technical nature since it had to contain an auditorium capable of seating an audience of 4200, a hotel, and an office building which were to finance the auditorium space. All this had to be fitted into a small parcel of valuable real estate, and furthermore, there were the structural problems that resulted from the auditorium's need for a large, column-free space.

When Wright joined the firm, the practice was housed on the top floor of the Borden Block in Randolph Street, the building itself an Adler and Sullivan design from 1880. When the Auditorium was completed in 1889, however, the firm soon moved into their magnificent new offices in the loft of the great tower. Wright not only had his own office, but it adjoined and was the same size as Sullivan's. This move from junior draftsman to something little short of an actual partner in the firm, is a further indication of Wright's rapid rise to fame.

During and after the construction of the Transportation Building, built for the Chicago World's Fair of 1893, it seems that Wright made several trips to the Fair. From the vast array of assembled exhibition pieces, the two that were to have the most lasting influences were the Pre-

Louis Henry Sullivan (1856-1924), the Chicago-based architect, was one of America's most advanced designers. Wright was apprenticed to him from 1887 until 1893, when Sullivan discovered Wright's independent, or 'bootleg,' commissions.

Columbian architecture of the reconstruction of the Mayan Nunnery of Uxmal and the Japanese *Ho-o-den*, a half-scale replica of a Fujiwara-period wooden temple. Coincidentaly, the *Ho-o-den*, and the treasures contained within it, were the first large-scale introduction to Mid-Western America of Japanese art and design. The fashion for Japonisme that had been cultivated in Europe since the 1860s by artists such as Whistler had slowly filtered through to the more avant-garde Americans. Wright's interest in the oriental had already been sparked by Silsbee who had collected 'orientalia.'

Despite an unmistakable kinship between Japanese architecture and some of Wright's own buildings, Wright was adamant that Japanese art and design did not influence him in the least. Refusing to acknowledge any influence from the east, Wright stated that Japanese art was simply an enjoyable pleasure.

In 1889 Wright's association with Adler and Sullivan had been formalized by a five-year contract which, although it bound Wright's services to the firm, also allowed for certain financial advantages since Wright had met a young woman, Catherine Tobin, whom he wished to marry. In order to have the funds to allow him to arrange his private life and, importantly for Wright, to allow him to build his own house at Oak Park, the contract allowed Wright to draw advances on his salary.

Paradoxically, it was to be this contract that ultimately dissolved Sullivan and Wright's relationship: as Wright's ambitions grew, so did his family, and faced with ever-increasing debts he undertook several domestic commissions on the side. One commission led to another, and he designed around nine buildings that he called his 'Bootlegged Houses,' including houses for George Blossom, and Thomas and Walter Gale; although they were not direct violations of his contract, knowledge of them was nevertheless withheld from Sullivan.

During the day Wright worked on the firm's commissions, but at night and at weekends, he supplemented his income with these bootleg works. Undoubtedly the pressure of the workload was influential to the design of these houses. In his memoirs, *An Autobiography*, Wright apologized for many of the buildings' 'Sullivanisms.' On closer inspection, however, it is possible to see the tell-tale signs that identify the work of Frank Lloyd Wright.

In the spring of 1893, Sullivan discovered the bootleg commissions and following a violent argument, Wright walked out of the office. The contract between the two lapsed but it took Wright some years to extricate the deeds to his own house at Oak Park from Sullivan's office. Wright would not see Sullivan again for nearly twenty years.

For Wright, designing and constructing the best possible buildings was a continuous process. Never satisfied, he constantly changed his designs and refined his ideas, even during the actual construction of the buildings. His continual re-evaluation of a design to find even better solutions is best seen at his own home at Oak Park. For the twenty years that he lived there (1889-1909), the Oak Park House served as the laboratory for Wright's experiments. In 1898 a studio was built adjoining the house and this too underwent constant changes. Rooms were enlarged or added, ceilings heightened, the arrangement of the windows changed, interior partitions moved and the entry route into the house modified. Wright even allowed for the growth of a willow tree to be uninterrupted by placing a hole in the roof of the studio.

The plan of the studio was a movement towards Wright's goal of free-flowing interior space where the function of various spaces (rather than rooms that were fixed) was defined by the bearing walls, chimneys, and occasional supports. The space within a house could now be changed to function according to the changing needs of the occupants. From 1893 to 1909, this home and studio at Oak Park

were at the center of his activities. In addition to the Oak Park studio, however, Wright also leased an office on the top floor of the Schiller Building in Randolph Street in downtown Chicago, for meetings with prominent clients like William Winslow and Nathan Moore.

This photograph shows Wright around 1904, a time when his independent career was beginning to flourish.

During the last few years of the nineteenth century Wright's studio experienced a quiet period with few major or noteworthy commissions. The new century, however, was to bring about a reawakening of creativity in general throughout the world, and in 1900 commissions began to pour steadily into the studio.

Confident that he was capable of transforming his approach to architecture into realized buildings, in 1901 Wright gave a lecture at Chicago's celebrated Hull House called *The Art and Craft of the Machine*, in which he spoke of the important role that new technology should play in any new architecture for America. To add weight to his words, in the same year Wright unveiled his plans for the Prairie House in two model houses drawn for the Curtis Publishing Company of Philadelphia. The first design, *A Home in a Prairie Town* (cost $7000), was unlike any typical American house, which was seen by Wright as essentially one big box outside with little boxes inside. Wright's designs for the Prairie House broke open the box allowing for

YE'VE LEFT A GLIMMER STILL TO CHEER
THE MAN~THE ARTIFEX
THAT HOLDS IN SPITE O'KNOCKS AND SCALE
O'FRICTION WASTE AN' SLIP.
AN' BY THAT LIGHT~ NOW MARK MY WORD~
WE'LL BUILD THE PERFECT SHIP.

physical and visual movement between inside and outside. The 'box' was opened up by the use of what Wright called 'light screens,' long bands of continuous windows, so that from inside the vista was totally unblocked. The cramped interior box-like rooms disappeared when Wright removed the fixed interior partitioning walls. Instead of walls Wright used head-height screens, arrangements of piers, and built-in furniture to create a series of interlocking spaces that indicated, without compartmentalizing, the possible use for each space. The result was that often the ground floor was a single space that embraced all the functions of living rooms, dining rooms, and libraries.

The second design, *A Small House with Lots of Room in It* (cost $5800), depended on a series of low gables rather than the more usual low-hipped roof for its external effect. This use of gables was to continue on and off in Wright's designs until 1906 when they were abandoned.

Opposite: The drafting room of the Frank Lloyd Wright Home and Studio, Oak Park, IL, 1889-1909. This was the first of Wright's top-lit, open-plan workrooms. This view shows the balcony suspended

on chains, and the quotation, of which Wright was very fond, which here is from Kipling. **Right:** General view of the Frank Lloyd Wright Home and Studio, Oak Park, IL, 1889-1909.

Despite the nationwide publicity that the drawings had, there was little or no immediate effect in America at large, which at the time was enjoying a vogue for the Mission House and California Bungalow styles of architecture. No commissions came into the studio as a direct result of the model houses and Wright's activity, for the time being anyway, was limited to the areas in and around Chicago.

The first of the real houses was to be erected for brothers-in-law Harley Bradley and Warren Hickox in Kankakee, Illinois. Following these houses came a succession of Prairie House commissions including the Willit, Fricke, Davenport, Thomas, Dana, Martin, and Beachy Houses.

In addition to the buildings themselves, Wright was often entrusted to design all the furnishings of the house including the carpets, drapery, light fixtures, and furniture. The finest example of this type of activity was in the Dana House, Wright's most extravagent commission of the period. Later, during Wright's stay in Europe, he produced a monograph *Ausgefuehrte Barten und Entwuerfe von Frank Lloyd Wright*, published in Berlin by Ernst Wasmuth in 1910. In this monograph Wright described the Dana House as one designed to accommodate the owners' art collection and for extensive entertaining. Completed in 1904 after a two-year building program, the Dana House was

on the site of an old Lawrence residence dating from the time when the family had been pioneer settlers in central Illinois. By the twentieth century, Susan Lawrence Dana was a leading socialite in the Springfield community and demanded a house more suited to her position.

The beauty of the Prairie House concept was its adaptability. It could be simple or complex in plan, be one story or more, be durable and made of stone, or constructed with a lightweight wooden frame. It was equally suited to the wide open spaces of the American Mid-West prairies as to the lawns of suburban areas, where in fact, they were mostly built.

The years between 1905 and 1910 were the heyday of the Prairie House: nearly two-thirds of all the work Wright designed, some forty houses, were built in these years. The adaptability of the Prairie House allowed Wright continuously to revise his approaches, to the extent that we can see a type of house built on a very limited budget and using mass-production techniques and materials, medium-priced and average-size Prairie Houses that answered the needs of the average American family, and Prairie Houses which because of their size and quality place them in a luxury class of their own.

Despite the variations and possibilities that the Prairie House offered, Wright began to tire of its vocabulary since he was not interested in developing one single style. Wright sought change. His own home at Oak Park was in a constant state of flux, even in the smallest details: when his stationery was reprinted, Wright would change the paper, the design, and his logo.

Following swiftly on from the domestic projects Wright received the commission for the new administration building for the Larkin Company, a building to be used for the sole purpose of the organization of a huge mail-order business. Not content with just designing the building itself, Wright also provided the designs for the innovative metal

Below: Larkin Company Administration building, Buffalo, NY, 1903, demolished 1949-50. Among the innovative features of this mail-order business building, were plate glass, air conditioning, and metal furniture.

Opposite: View through the central atrium of the Larkin building.

furniture, filing cabinets, and lighting fixtures. Furthermore, the new building also contained one of the earliest forms of air-conditioning system.

The years up to 1909 were busy ones for Wright as he continued to extend his range of works from domestic houses into new areas such as shops, churches, and factories, and into new locations such as California. Nevertheless Wright had his full share of disappointments in major designs that remained unexecuted, and despite his achievements with the Prairie House, Wright wrote in his autobiography that now aged forty, he felt he was tired and lacking interest in his work.

In addition to the mental strain he was undergoing, there was also the added discord in his family life. His inability to budget or save meant that he was constantly short of money and by 1909, Wright and his wife were estranged. Like an action reply of his father's behavior in 1885, towards the end of October 1909 Wright abruptly left his family and business. After taking the train to New York, Wright sailed for Europe. He was, however, not alone: with him was the wife of a neighbor and client, Mrs Edwin Cheney. For two weeks the scandal was kept from the public but the news was eventually broken on November 7th by the front page of the Chicago Tribune. For two years there was to be no further news of Frank Lloyd Wright except for the knowledge that he and Mrs Cheney were living quietly in a villa in Fièsole near Florence.

For the two years of Wright's absence, his practice and commissions were supervised from the office of German-born architect Herrmann Von Holst by Marion Mahoney, one of the first women to graduate from MIT and the first licenced woman architect in Illinois, and her husband Walter Burley Griffin, whose greatest single work was the plan of the city of Canberra, the Australian federal capital. On his return to the United States, socially and professionally shunned in Chicago, Wright re-established his practice at Taliesin, his summer home at Spring Green, Wisconsin.

During the summer of 1914, while Wright was in Chicago, Taliesin was destroyed: a crazed cook set fire to the building, destroying important documents and records of Wright's early work, and killing most of the inhabitants, including Mrs Cheney. At 45 years old, Wright was, incredibly, able to come to terms with this personal tragedy.

In 1917 Wright shifted his work-base once more, moving from Chicago/Taliesin to Los Angeles. When he was absent from Los Angeles, Wright's projects were executed by his son Lloyd Wright and an assistant Rudolph Schindler (1887-1953), a graduate of the Vienna Academy of Fine Arts. Schindler, however, like Wright had once done, took advantage of Wright's absences to start his own practice.

The major attractions that Southern California had for Wright were that for him the area had the sense of being a desert that could be changed, in the first instance by adding water, and later by introducing planned cities. Furthermore, the area was related both factually and mythically to a primitive pre-Columbian culture. The land itself also spread itself out with that horizontality so beloved of Wright. Wright had, in fact, designed his first building in California in 1909, the George C Stewart House in Montecito, a two-story cruciform Prairie House successfully transplanted to a Pacific-coastal environment.

For fifty years Wright would design for California, continuing in some instances to employ many Prairie-house elements until they were gradually absorbed into his later attempts at new forms of regional architecture.

The second significant phase of Wright's career was brought about after he had completed the last concrete block house in Tulsa, Oklahoma, in 1929, and by the first of his projects to exploit to the limits the possibilities of concrete cantilevers.

Since 1901 in his address *The Art and Craft of the Machine* Wright realized that the machine age was destined to bring about great changes in the nature of civilization, but it was not until the 1920s that he assembled entire buildings from mass-produced elements like concrete blocks. Forced by the economic climate of America in the depression years of the 1930s, Wright realized the limits of traditional materials and construction techniques. In abandonning the Prairie style, Wright would create an architecture of concrete armatures and glass exteriors.

From 1936, in the depths of the great Depression until

Charles Ennis House, Los Angeles, CA, 1923. This was the last of Wright's four 'textile-block' houses, surfaced in blocks with a repetitive, geometrical pattern.

his death in 1959, Wright continued to develop his Uso-nian Houses, another scheme for moderate-cost housing. Built of brick, wood, and glass which was used inside and outside, the flat-roofed houses were designed to open out on to private gardens through glazed doors. And although they were designed initially for clients with limited budgets but who appreciated fine design, often the principles of the Usonian houses were used by Wright for his wealthier clients.

The two most famous of Wright's buildings of this period, the Edgar Kauffmann House at Bear Run in Penn-sylvania, better known as *Fallingwater*, and the Administra-tion Building for the Johnson Wax Company in Racine, Wisconsin, form the poles of Wright's attempts at creating 'total environments.' Ever since his work on the Martin House and the Larkin Building of 1904, Wright had striven to assimilate home building with the processes of nature and the building of work places to the ideas of the sacra-ment. For Wright the hearth in the home was the moral and spiritual center while in the workplace, by the

Above; The Rayward-Shepherd House, New Canaan, CT, 1955.

Right: Interior of Fallingwater, Bear Run, PA, 1936. Wright built this ultimate expression of the Usonian House for Edgar Kaufmann, Snr.

Above and Opposite: Scenes during the building of Wright's home and studio, Taliesin West, Scottsdale, AZ, 1940. The photographs were taken by Pedro Guerrero who was Wright's photographer from this time until his death in 1959.

use of well-placed inscriptions (like the one in the entrance to the Larkin building which read: 'Honest Labor needs no master, simple justice needs no slaves'), the 'sacred' could be projected into it.

By 'Usonian,' Wright meant something altogether more modest than *Fallingwater*: open-planned, small houses designed for convenience, economy, and comfort.

In his autobiography Wright set down a number of design-features that were essential to his Usonian idea. Gone were visible roofs for they were expensive and unnecessary. So too was furniture, pictures, and bric-a-brac because he believed that the walls of the buildings could be made to include them, or even *be* them. The term 'Usonian' thus meant far more than simply a description of a small single-story house: Usonian for Wright was synonymous with the 'organic,' the democratic, and the demographic. The creation of Usonian houses paradoxically, however, depended entirely on that combination of architect and trusting client.

Above: In his final years Wright investigated the possibilities of prefabricated buildings.

Right and Opposite: Wright's final masterpiece was the Solomon R Guggenheim Museum in New York. Its basic structural form was a shallow-spiraling ramp, which gives both the interior and the exterior a highly futuristic appearance.

In addition to the spatial organization of the Usonian house, Wright introduced three new construction techniques. Firstly, the walls of the Usonian House were made of composite panels, easy to install and which did away with the added expense in time and money of finishing and decorating them. Secondly, these panels were laid out on a grid system which controlled the entire plan and also allowed for a certain amount of prefabrication. Finally, Wright introduced light-weight cast floor-slabs which carried steam and hot water pipes for underfloor heating. With this Wright eliminated the under-utilized basement area and provided continuous heating without awkward radiators, making floor-to-ceiling windows and glazed doors possible.

But the building which must be regarded as the climax of Wright's career is the Solomon R Guggenheim Museum in New York. With its internal spiraling gallery which Wright compared to an unbroken wave, the museum combined all the structural and spatial principles and achievements that had concerned Wright throughout his 75 years as a practicing architect.

EARLY WORK

The hand of Joseph Lyman Silsbee's newest apprentice, Frank Lloyd Wright, is first seen in the design for a house for property-developer J L Cochrane. The pen and ink perspective is neatly lettered *F L Wright, Del*, and it is interesting to note that Wright's approach to rendering details such as the plants and trees surrounding the house is in a stylized manner that was to be adopted by other draftsmen in Silsbee's office.

Not content with a few designs for Silsbee's commissions, Wright soon began expressing his own ideas about design in independent projects. In the early summer of 1887 Wright's design for the Unitarian Chapel for Sioux City, Iowa was published in the *Inland Architect and News Record* (Vol 9, June 1887). The design reflects some of Silsbee's own approach: from the outside it retained the informal clubhouse appearance of All Souls' Church with a Shingle Style circular alcove and cupola. Inside, however, the space could be divided by moveable screens, Wright's first attempts at breaking down the established attitudes towards compartmentalizing space. Furthermore, the broad, oblong, leaded sash windows were the forerunners of the type that Wright would use in later projects like the Winslow House and in the early designs of the Oak Park period.

In the same year, Wright also undertook the design of the Hillside Home School at Spring Green, where his maiden aunts Jane and Nell Lloyd-Jones were experimenting in teaching. With Silsbee's assistance on the practical problems of design, the project continued on and off for several years with the supervision of the project transferred between Wright and Silsbee on several occasions.

Moreover, most of the domestic buildings constructed after 1887 by Adler and Sullivan were the work of Frank Lloyd Wright. While the business was ably looked after by Adler, Sullivan was able to concentrate on the problems presented by offices and commercial buildings while his young assistant Wright took care of the 'domestic' side of the business. From 1887 to 1893, during the period in which Wright worked for the firm, Adler and Sullivan designed and constructed nine houses. Two houses completed in 1887 were already under construction when Wright joined, but from the beginning of 1888, Wright appears to have had overall control, both administratively and as a designer, of the remaining seven projects.

By the summer of 1891 Wright had firmly established his importance. In the same year the firm also published the preliminary drawings of the commission for the Transportation Building for the *Chicago World's Fair* in 1893.

The Transportation Building was a vast empty hall, large enough to house the display of railway engines, carriages, and the latest development in transportation, the automobile. The structure of the building posed several problems which were ultimately solved by Adler, while the great entrance, The Golden Gate, the most remarkable and memorable feature of the building with its oriental-inspired surface decoration, was the work of Wright and Sullivan.

Soon after Wright established his downtown office, William H Winslow, the president of a company of architectural ironmongers, came to him with the commission for a new house in River Forest, a suburb lying to the west of Oak Park. With its hip roof and wide eaves reminiscent of Japanese architecture, the Winslow House was the forerunner of Wright's Prairie Houses which would make their appearance in the early years of the twentieth century.

In the early 1890s the New England Colonial style of architecture was making its first appearance in the Mid-West and the Blossom House was Wright's working of the revived style. Although the house was complete with yellow clapboard, white trim, a classical portico, and Palladian windows, the early Wrightian touches of the hip roof that is flatter than the original style demanded, the oblong sash windows, and the arrangement of interior space are evident.

In 1892 Wright designed three houses for Walter H Gale. One was Gale's own house (later sold to his brother Thomas), while the remaining two houses were built for speculation. A year later Walter Gale commissioned a further house at 1031 Chicago Avenue at Oak Park. Recalling the principal motif of Silsbee's All Souls' Church, in the second Walter Gale House, Wright used a two-story semi-circular bay juxtaposed with a two-story dormer window. Inside, the arrangement of rooms is a practical solution for a small house, although it is still one of compartmentalized space. Wright was still some way off from his ultimate goal of free-flowing interiors. But in his

The Frank Lloyd Wright Home
and Studio, 1889-1909
Oak Park, IL
Drafting Room
Photo, Jon Miller, © Hedrich-Blessing

attempts to bring the 'inside outside,' the wide open verandah that fronts the house was the first step.

After setting himself up in independent practice in 1893, although his work still bore traces of the influence of Silsbee and Sullivan, Wright began to develop and concentrate on his principles for a new architecture. The first major commission at the time of his independence came from William H Winslow for a new house in River Forest. Winslow had acquired a large piece of property in Auvergne Place, a private road that had been cut through the Waller Estate, a wooded and flat area of land through which flowed the Desplaines River.

The area was the perfect setting for the Prairie house which is what the Winslow House was to be. Harmonizing with its level woodland setting, the Winslow House's most important innovation is the low hip roof with its projecting eaves. Wright was attempting to make the house 'part of the land' emphasizing the function of the building as a shelter. The low roof, reminiscent of traditional Japanese architecture, furthermore removed all possibility of using the attics as living spaces, and thus Wright moved household servants out of dark cramped quarters into new areas.

The leitmotif of the Winslow House is the horizontal line: the low hip roof projects over walls made up of a lower band of brick and an upper band of colored tiles. The horizontal is further emphasized in the wide, oblong windows, the broad, low chimney, and the shallow central steps up to the low terrace. But Sullivan's influence can be detected in the abstract motif of oak leaves in the gypsum plaster frieze on the second story and in the design of the carved oak door which expresses Sullivan's ideas of natural, organic growth as the basis for good design.

Not all of Wright's clients would accept such revolutionary designs: Nathan Moore came to Wright in 1894 with a commission for an 'English' house, complete with mock-Tudor timbering. The Nathan Moore house would enjoy wide acclaim and Wright reported that he frequently had to turn away clients who wanted similar houses. The experience of working in the medieval style did however lead Wright to design a scheme for townhouses, a set of four houses for Robert W Roloson in Chicago. Roloson owned property on Chicago's South Side which he wanted to improve, and Wright's plans for the Roloson Houses were a new approach to the problem of providing a row of four identical houses that would not only fit into the crowded area of the city but whose leases would provide Roloson with a return on his investment.

The buildings were planned on the mezzanine principle where there is a difference in the floor heights between rooms at the front of the building and the rooms at the back. The break in the floor level occurs at the large central stairwell. Although there are touches of Sullivanesque ornament, the interiors have a geometrical quality that is essentially Wrightian, as do the exteriors, with their great gables.

One of the last important domestic commissions of the last decade of the nineteenth century for Wright was the Isidore Heller House at South Woodlawn Avenue, Chicago. On a small city lot on the South Side of the city, the Heller House sports a type of roof known as 'monitor,' where a third smaller story with its own hipped roof is added above the main eaves of the roof over the two lower storeys. The walls of the third story only partly enclose the space and are decorated with a Sullivanesque ornamental frieze broken by the open arcades. The central feature of each panel of the frieze is a human figure in high relief and is the work of Richard Bock, an Oak Park sculptor who collaborated with Wright on many occasions. Beautiful as this loggia is, it is somewhat out of place on a house in a city street, nor is there any real view to be enjoyed from it. Inside the house, however, the two main areas of living and dining rooms are in a cruciform shape that Wright would use frequently in the Prairie Houses. Corresponding to the arms of the cross within are the short rectangular projections of the wall outside.

In 1895 Wright undertook the designs for multiple dwelling or apartment houses. The first of these, the Francis Apartment, were built in Chicago for the Terre Haute Trust Company of Indiana, the second was an Edward Waller project, Francisco Terrace, located in the heavily populated district of Chicago known as the 'near West side.' The Francisco Terrace was, in effect, a model tenement, two stories high and constructed around the four sides of a rectangular central courtyard. Along the street sides of the rectangle (the two longer sides), the building is doubly thick to contain pairs of apartments. The apartments facing the street were accessible from the sidewalks while those overlooking the courtyard had their access through a single wide archway, opening the courtyard to the street at its narrow end. At each corner of the block were open towers containing the public stairways serving the overhanging gallery that is the walkway to the front doors of the upper-story apartments. Despite the advantages of direct entry to each apartment from the outside, the disadvantages of the plan included lack of privacy and the noise from the wooden gallery and the courtyard which reverberated through the building. In fact the secret of the early success of the Francisco Terrace project was that at first it housed only young (and so far childless) couples, something that led the development to be known as 'Honeymoon Court.'

Once again the Sullivanesque touches are evident in the decorative details: the spandrels of the terracotta archway at the entrance to the courtyard (removed in 1977 and replaced on a restored building at Lake Street and Euclid Avenue at Oak Park) are filled with folliage reminiscent of Wright and Sullivan's Golden Gate portal for the Transportation Building of 1893.

The George Blossom
Residence, 1892
Chicago, IL
Photo, © Wayne Andrews/Esto

Above: Frank Lloyd Wright Home and Studio
Exterior of drafting room
Photo, Jon Miller, © Hedrich Blessing

Left: Frank Lloyd Wright Home and Studio, 1889-1909
Oak Park, IL
Studio entrance
Photo, Jon Miller, © Hedrich Blessing

Opposite: Frank Lloyd Wright Home and Studio
Octagonal Library
Photo, Jon Miller, © Hedrich Blessing

Above: Frank Lloyd Wright
Home and Studio
Playroom looking east, mural
by Orlando Giannini
*Photo, Jon Miller, © Hedrich
Blessing*

Opposite: Frank Lloyd Wright
Home and Studio
Playroom at east end
*Photo, Jon Miller, © Hedrich
Blessing*

27

Above: Frank Lloyd Wright
Home and Studio
View into the living room
*Photo, Jon Miller, © Hedrich
Blessing*

Opposite: Frank Lloyd Wright
Home and Studio
Dining Room
*Photo, Jon Miller, © Hedrich
Blessing*

Opposite: Frank Lloyd Wright
Home and Studio
Living Room with fireplace
inglenook
*Photo, Jon Miller, © Hedrich
Blessing*

Above: Frank Lloyd Wright
Home and Museum
Master Bedroom
*Photo, Jon Miller, © Hedrich
Blessing*

William H Winslow
Residence, 1893
River Forest, IL
*Photo, Bill Crofton, courtesy of
the Frank Lloyd Wright Home
and Studio*

The Harem, 1901
(The Frank Wright Thomas
Residence)
Oak Park, IL
Photo, © Balthazar Korab

William G Fricke Residence,
1901
Oak Park, IL
Photo, © Balthazar Korab

Above: Francisco Terrace
Apartments, 1895
Chicago, IL
Demolished, 1974
Photo, © Wayne Andrews/Esto

Opposite: Nathan G Moore
Residence, 1895
Oak Park, IL
Photo, © Balthazar Korab

THE PRAIRIE HOUSE

The first Prairie Houses that were erected were in Kankakee, Illinois for Harley Bradley and his brother-in-law Warren Hickox in 1900. These houses had the low, broad-gabled roofs, similar in appearance to the *Small House with Lots of Room in It*, which he unveiled in Chicago in 1901, but were far more 'tailormade' in their details and their fittings. Following their construction a number of commissions followed and a host of Prairie Houses were erected by 1904, including the Ward W Willet House, the William G Fricke House, the E Arthur Davenport House, the Frank W Thomas House, the Susan Lawrence Dana House, the Arthur Heurtley House, the W E Martin House and the Peter A Beachey House. All share the same broad principles of the mature Prairie Houses in their flowing plans, reduced story-heights, and geometrical ornamentations.

The finest example of Wright's Prairie Houses is the Dana House in Springfield, Illinois. It is roofed with low, broad gables and the plan of the house is roughly a 'T' shape, with the largest 'arm' extended by a pergola which contained the family's art collection. The exterior color provided by the buff-colored bricks and bronze lustered tiles is reflected inside the house in its furnishings of browns, russets and golds. Overall the decorative scheme unites the exterior and interior architecture: the exterior ornamental frieze incorporates a highly stylized motif of prairie flora, such as sumac, a native Illinois plant. This motif is repeated in the leaded glass windows and, again inside, more naturalistically, in the painted mural by George Niedecken.

The variety possible with the Prairie House formula is seen in two of these types: the Coonley House and the Robie House. Both were the product of that rare and magical mix of an avant-garde designer and a liberal and trusting client. They left everything in the capable hands of Frank Lloyd Wright.

Based on a centrifugal plan over a raised basement, all the principal rooms in the Coonley House (except the centrally located children's playroom) are on the second level and each room looks out over the lawns and garden from a specified height. Yet due to Wright's 'horizontal' style, the exterior of the house betrays little sense of height. Built with a U-shaped plan using a frame construction, the exterior walls have a banded effect due to the lower parts having a surface of fine sand plaster, while the upper part of the walls are faced with geometrically patterned tiles.

Inside the Coonley House the space is arranged laterally in large sweeping vistas while the height of the ceilings has been lowered to more human scale. The harmonious shapes and textures are again the work of Wright who designed all the furnishings and fittings.

In contrast, the Robie House in Woodland Avenue on Chicago's South Side, was a city house built on an average-sized city lot. Unlike the Coonley House, the Robie House is a building whose volumes are arranged along a single axis and constructed of heavy brickwork and concrete. Also, perhaps for the first time in American architecture, the Robie House boasts an integral garage. Nicknamed the 'Battleship,' the various levels of the Robie House have been seen as decks and its projecting terraces as prows.

Inside the spaces that require a certain degree of privacy – the bedroom, kitchen, and servants' quarters – are placed at the rear of the house. The living room, central stairwell, and dining room are perceived as a single unit, separated but not divided by the chimney. There is not a single dividing wall or partition and the space extends into two diamond-shaped bays at each end, which in turn open on to porches. In fact each major space has direct access to the outside. But because it is a city house, the outside had been constructed: instead of open country, Wright provided porches and balconies.

In all, the Robie House confounds all our expectations of what a house should look like: there is no street façade, no obvious door, and hardly any solid walls. The distinguishing feature, by which we can instantly recognize the house, is the famous roof, cantilevered and extending twenty feet beyond the masonry supports. Shunning any intricate ornamentation or historical details in favor of straight horizontal lines, the Robie House stands in sharp contrast to its neighbors that were themselves built only ten years before.

Frederick C Robie Residence,
1906
Chicago, IL
Living Room
Photo, Jon Miller, © Hedrich Blessing

Above: The Dana-Thomas
Residence, 1902
Springfield, IL
*Photo, David Paul Blanchette,
Illinois Historic Preservation
Agency*

Left: The Dana-Thomas
Residence
Butterfly chandelier
*Photo, David Paul Blanchette,
Illinois Historic Preservation
Agency*

Opposite above: The Dana-
Thomas Residence
Sumac window
*Photo, David Paul Blanchette,
Illinois Historic Preservation
Agency*

Opposite right: The Dana-
Thomas Residence
Detail, exterior frieze
*Photo, David Paul Blanchette,
Illinois Historic Preservation
Agency*

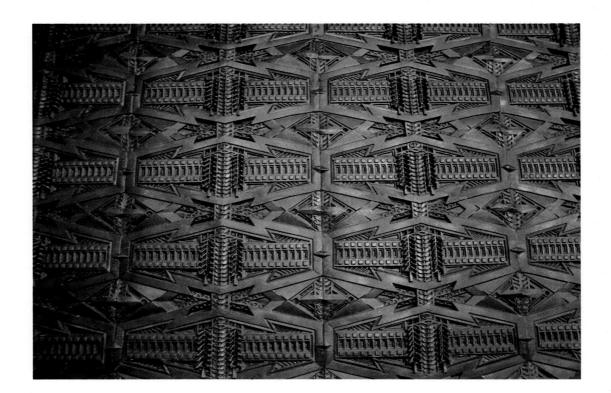

Darwin D Martin Residence,
1904
Buffalo, NY
Photo, © Balthazar Korab

Arthur Heurtley Residence,
1902
Oak Park, IL
Photo, © Balthazar Korab

Unity Temple, 1904
Oak Park, IL
Interior
*Photo, Bill Crofton, courtesy of
the Frank Lloyd Wright Home
and Studio*

Unity Temple
Photo, © Balthazar Korab

Frederick C Robie Residence,
1906
Chicago, IL
Photo, Jon Miller, © Hedrich-Blessing

Meyer May Residence, 1908
Grand Rapids, MI
Photo, © Balthazar Korab

Above: Meyer May Residence
Hall with hollyhock mural by
George Neidecken
Photo, courtesy of Steelcase, Inc.

Opposite: Meyer May
Residence
Living Room
Photo, © Balthazar Korab

Above: Meyer May Residence
Living room with fireplace
Photo, courtesy of Steelcase, Inc.

Opposite: Meyer May
Residence
Morning Room
Photo, courtesy of Steelcase, Inc.

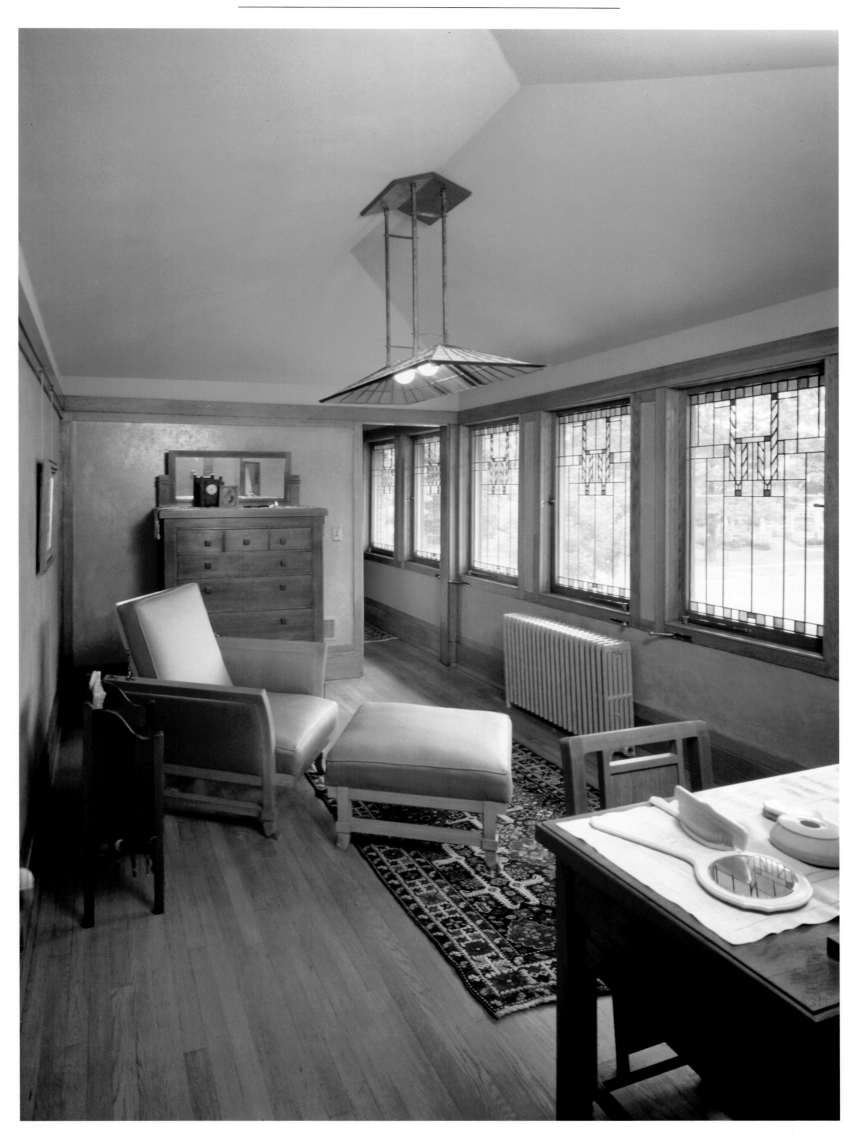

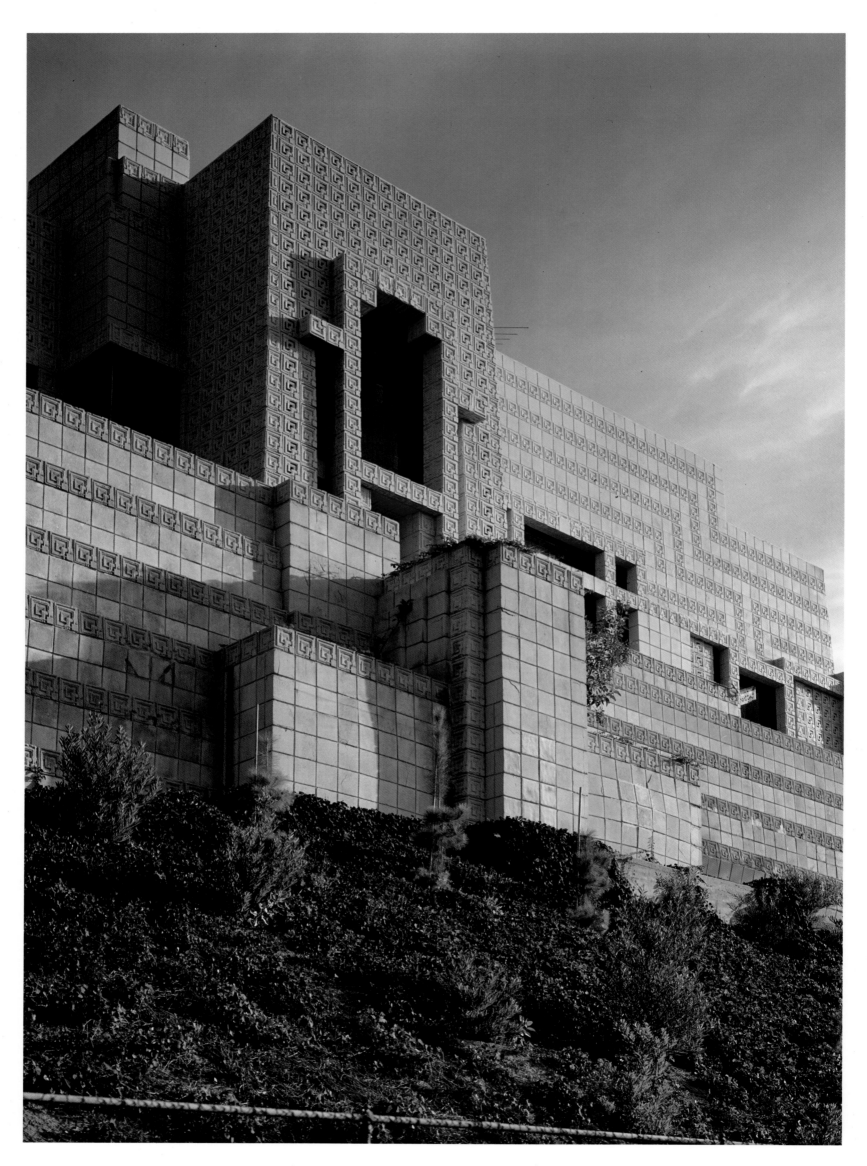

Influences and New Materials

In the late summer of 1913 Wright was approached by Edward Waller Jnr, with a commission to create an entertainment center on Cottage Green Avenue, Chicago. Modeled on the outdoor garden restaurants popular in Germany, Wright's Midway Gardens was an architectural complex for indoor and outdoor dining, dancing, and concerts. As well as designing the building itself, Wright was also responsible for the design of all the furnishings and even details like the tableware, the designs for which were based on the Vienna Secessionist abstract principles and motifs that he had no doubt encountered during his European sojourn.

By 1914 Wright had completed work on Midway Gardens, the last concerted work in Chicago of his design team. The next major project, one of Wright's greatest architectural achievements, was the Imperial Hotel in Tokyo. Like Midway Gardens, the Imperial Hotel was a large complex that was unified by Wright's working of the decorative scheme that included the design of all the interior details – furniture, carpets, ceramics, silverware, and textiles. Wright also utilized traditional Japanese masonry by using castellated profiles constructed in brick dressed in Oya; a sort of lava-stone. In addition to this, Wright used terracotta on the exterior and interior arcades of the hotel to give a rich mosaic-like effect, similar to that achieved at Midway Gardens. The construction of the Imperial Hotel began in 1916 and continued until 1922, during which time Wright was frequently in Japan to supervise the work. Back home, Wright's commissions included prefabricated buildings in Milwaukee designed for the Arthur Richards Company using pre-cut timber and assembled into various designs. Many of these buildings were constructed throughout the Mid-West and are now identified as Wright's American Readicut buildings.

In 1917 Wright moved from Chicago to Los Angeles. The most widely known of Wright's West Coast designs is the Aline Barnsdall House, better-known as the Hollyhock House. The concrete house, built high on a hill in Hollywood, with its stylized patterns of hollyhocks and mass of smooth masonry reflects Wright's interest in pre-European, pre-Columbian forms, in this case Mayan architecture. The main public areas of the house, the music and living rooms which overlook the square pool, together with library, are arranged in the classic Wrightian T-shape, a device he frequently used in the Mid-Western Prairie Houses of the early 1900s. Here, however, he added two extended wings which enclose the garden court and a walled patio area. But once again the entrance to the Hollyhock House is a strange affair: it is between the dining and music rooms through a long loggia.

Since the turn of the century, Wright and other avant-garde architects had proposed concrete, concrete block, and cement stucco sheathing as new materials for domestic architecture. The combined house and book studio for Alice Millard, designed and built in the early 1920s, was Wright's first textured concrete block house in California. Situated in a valley surrounded by trees and overlooking a pond, La Miniatura has a two-story living room with a 'window wall' of glass doors at the lower level and pierced concrete blocks above. The thin concrete blocks with a cross pattern suggested by the pre-Columbian architecture at Oaxaca in Mexico occur both on the external walls and inside. The construction of the building used what Wright called a 'knitblock' system, where two parallel rows of four-inch-thick concrete blocks (made with sand from the site to produce a color and texture that was in keeping with the location), with an air cavity between the two rows, were knitted together and reinforced by steel rods.

The Storer House was Wright's second textured concrete block house, the design of which with its central high living room appears like a rectangle with low wings to each side. In addition to the building whose construction Wright supervised, he also acted as the landscape architect, the idea being that the whole building should appear like a ruin hidden in a jungle.

The last of Wright's concrete block houses of the 1920s in California, the Freeman House, was also the smallest. In a way not usually associated with concrete, Wright produced a house that was light and airy by using perforated blocks with set-in glass. Once again the range of historical influences is apparent, but this time the pre-Columbian is mixed with Islamic motifs, such as in the use of perforated screens instead of heavy masonary walls, a method reminiscent of Islamic architecture.

Charles Ennis Residence, 1923
Los Angeles, CA
Photo, © Balthazar Korab

Above: Imperial Hotel, 1915
Tokyo, Japan
Demolished, 1968
Photo, UPI/Bettmann

Opposite above: Imperial
Hotel
Photo, UPI/Bettmann

Opposite below: Chair for
Imperial Hotel
The Cooper-Hewitt Museum
The Smithsonian Institution

Top: Hollyhock House, 1917
(The Aline Barnsdall
Residence)
Los Angeles, CA
Photo, Virginia Ernst Kazor

Above: Charles Ennis
Residence, 1923
Los Angeles, CA
Façade detail
Photo, © Balthazar Korab

John Storer Residence, 1923
Hollywood, CA
Photo, © Balthazar Korab

Taliesin II, 1925-1959
Spring Green, WI
Photo, © Ezra Stoller/Esto

Taliesin II
Photo, © Balthazar Korab

Taliesin II
Interior of the theater
Photo, © Balthazar Korab

Taliesin II
Photo, © Balthazar Korab

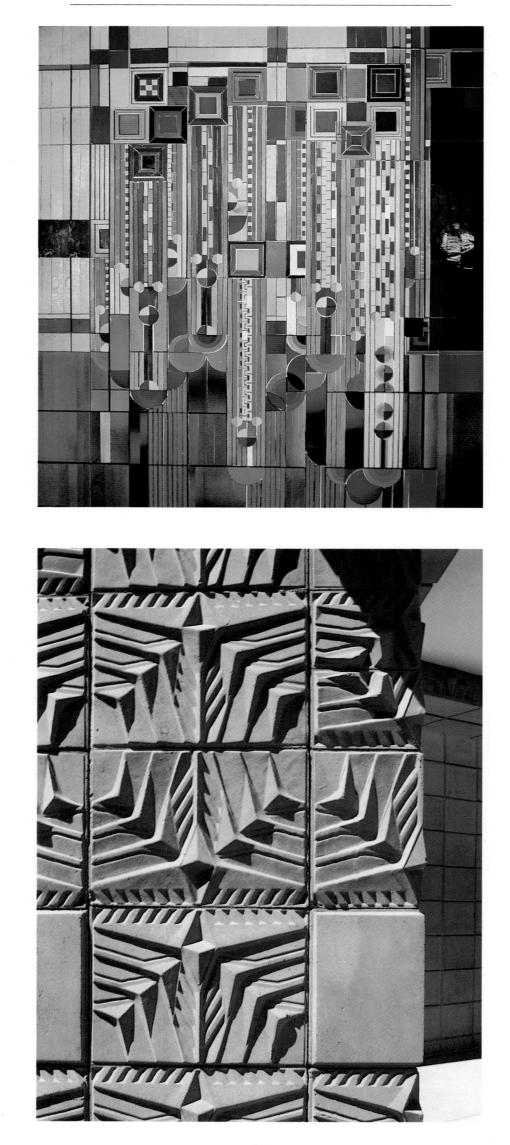

Above: Arizona Biltmore, 1927
Phoenix, AZ
Photo, © Balthazar Korab

Opposite above: Arizona
Biltmore
Glass mural – Grand lobby
Photo, © Balthazar Korab

Opposite below: Arizona
Biltmore
Façade detail
Photo, © Balthazar Korab

New Ideas and the Usonian House

When Frank Lloyd Wright described his buildings as 'organic' he meant that he used the concrete cantilever in a manner similar to the way a tree supports its canopy of branches. Nowhere is this better demonstrated than in the Administration Building for the Johnson Wax Co, Racine, Wisconsin. Wright's organic metaphor is displayed in the tall, slender lily-pad-capped columns that taper gently toward their bases and support the open-planned office. Between the 'lilypads' is a ceiling of glass tubing: the diffused light comes not through the walls where we would normally expect to find windows, but through the ceiling. Wright's formula of a large external box containing lots of small boxes inside it has been completely revised.

Wright's belief was that the employees' attention should be focused entirely on his 'sacred' work and not distracted by views through windows. This belief led him to create a self-contained, hermetic environment that physically excluded the outside world.

While this building represented Wright's interpretation of the sacramental place of work, his architectural masterpiece *Fallingwater* represents his ideal of a living-place fused with nature. Straddling a small stream called Bear Run, the house is rooted to a ledge of rock and projects out as a free-floating platform over a small waterfall. In this building, more than in any other, Wright broke with the 'box' format of traditional buildings by separating the horizontal and vertical planes. Concrete cantilevered planes are held together by walls of rough stone of different thickness, laid in alternating courses. Because it is so completely fused with the landscape and the ground on which it is built, no single photograph can ever completely record *Fallingwater*.

Ironically, Wright's attitude to concrete was somewhat ambivalent: although he acknowledged that it had made such a design feasible, he continued to regard concrete as a material with little inherent quality and had at first proposed covering the Kauffmann house with a layer of gold leaf. Eventually dissuaded by his client, Wright nevertheless finished the concrete surface in apricot paint.

Wright's first Usonian House was commissioned by Herbert and Katherine Jacobs in Madison, Wisconsin, in 1936.

They were clients who shared Wright's belief that good architecture was not necessarily beyond the means of the average American. Inside, the greatest innovation was Wright's juxtaposition of a kitchen area and a small dining area. By abolishing the dining room *per se* completely, the Usonian housewife could now watch her children playing outside, entertain visitors, and cook a meal at the same time.

Later clients for Usonian houses allowed Wright to demonstrate just how versatile the Usonian form was: each house was unique and could have a strict or extravagant budget; the grid could be L-shaped, rectangular, square, triangular, or even a hexagon and the plan could be varied depending on the client's needs and the building's site.

The Hanna House or the Honeycomb House as it is sometimes known, looks like a country house, despite its suburban location. The modular concept of this building is a repeated hexagon arranged like a honeycomb to produce an open plan and to project the various interior spaces outwards on to the terraces. Outside, brick has been used, but inside the thin walls are of layered and laminated wood that are moveable, allowing for the replacement and rearrangement of space as the family's needs changed.

Wright frequently elaborated on the theme of the Usonian House. Nearly always arranged around a tight, compact masonry core which often featured the fireplace (the sacred hearth) and the kitchen workspace, some of the houses were enlarged and spread out over their site, while others were detailed and designed so that the owners could build their own houses. An example of this is the Robert Berger House where even the family dog is provided with a Usonian kennel.

Another group of Wright's Usonian schemes from the post-World War II period are based on segments of a circle. The segmented circle design was first used in a second house for the Jacobs in 1944 and appears later in the Pearce House of 1950. The original L-shape of the Usonian House is transformed into a C-shape arrangement, where the concave area of the curve contains an outdoor courtyard living-space.

George D Sturges Residence,
1939
Brentwood Heights, CA
Photo, © Balthazar Korab

Above: Fallingwater, 1935
(The Edgar J Kaufmann, Sr.
Residence)
Bear Run, PA
Photo, © Balthazar Korab

Left: Fallingwater
Detail of Garden
*Photo, © Western Pennsylvania
Conservancy*

Top: Fallingwater
Exterior from the land side
*Photo, © Western Pennsylvania
Conservancy*

Above: Fallingwater
Living room
*Photo, © Western Pennsylvania
Conservancy*

Top: S C Johnson and Son
Administration Building, 1936,
and Research Tower, 1944
Racine, WI
Photo, courtesy of John Wax

Above: Desk and Chair for
Johnson Wax Administration
Building
Photo, courtesy of Steelcase, Inc.

70

Johnson Wax Administration
Building
Great Workroom in 1939
Photo, courtesy of John Wax

Wingspread, 1937
(The Herbert F Johnson
Residence)
Wind Point, WI
*Photo, courtesy of the Johnson
Foundation*

Opposite: Wingspread
Interior
Photo, © Balthazar Korab

Honeycomb House, 1936
(The Paul R Hanna
Residence)
Stanford, CA
Photo, © Balthazar Korab

Taliesin West, 1937-1959
Scottsdale, AZ
Photo, © Pedro E Guerrero

Above: Taliesin West
photo, © Pedro E Guerrero

Opposite: Taliesin West
Photo, © Pedro E Guerrero

Taliesin West
Interior
Photo, © Pedro E Guerrero

Taliesin West
Interior
Photo, © Pedro E Guerrero

Above: Annie Pfeiffer Chapel,
1938
Florida Southern College
Lakeland, FL
*Photo, courtesy of Florida
Southern College – M Thorn*

Opposite: Pfeiffer Chapel
Interior
*Photo, courtesy of Florida
Southern College*

Florida Southern College
Esplanades
Photo, courtesy of Florida
Southern College

Photo, courtesy of Florida
Southern College

FRANK LLOYD WRIGHT

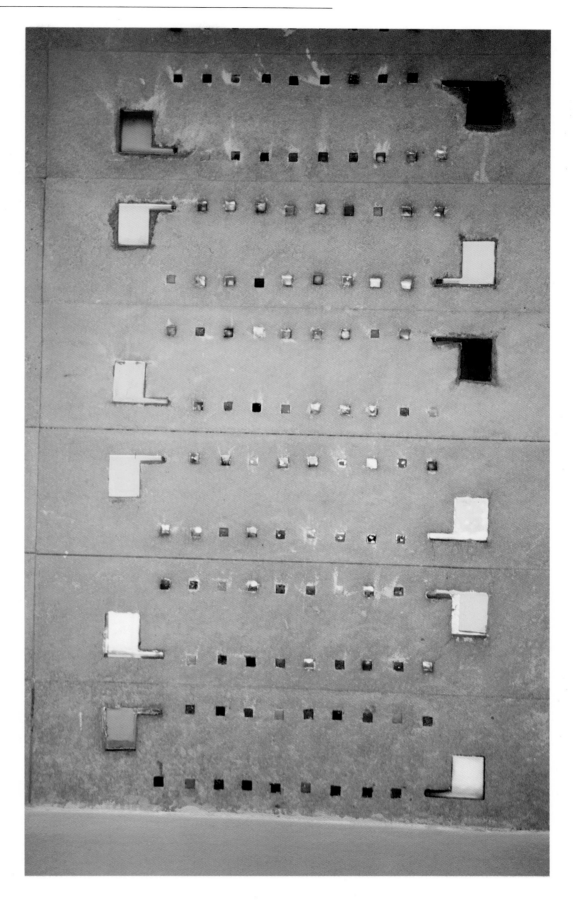

Florida Southern College
Detail of glass used in bricks
*Photo, courtesy of Florida
Southern College*

'THE NEXT ONE'

When, toward the end of his life, Frank Lloyd Wright was asked what his favorite building was, he answered simply, 'the next one.' His answer reflects the continuing process of refinement that he caused his work to undergo, not only during the initial design stages, but also in his habit of continually altering buildings during construction. Even after the buildings were complete, Wright continued to develop and improve the designs in his mind and in subsequent projects.

What was originally a plan for an apartment house, the unexecuted St Marks Tower in New York of 1929, was eventually realized in 1953 as the Harold C Price Company Tower in Bartlesville, Oklahoma. The 19-story office-apartment and cantilevered steel tower is based on a tree-like structure, and, like a tree in nature, the tower appears different from every direction. Wright also felt that sky-scrapers were unsuitable buildings for urban areas. In his vision, towers should stand free in open land. Continuing the forms developed in the Imperial Hotel project in Tokyo, Wright re-worked the hexagonal-backed chairs for the furniture of the Price Tower.

In addition to Wright's practical Usonian Houses, it has been noted that at the same time he was developing a more curious, theatrical, even 'sci-fi' type of architecture in the unbuilt Sports Club for Huntingdon, Hartford. Planned in 1947, the designs for this have been likened to a group of flying saucers moored to masonry masts, or even earlier still, in a sketch in 1925, for the Gordon Strong Planetarium. This project, though unbuilt, took the form of a zig-gurat with a spiraling car ramp on the outside. This spiral ramp would reappear in later projects, notably the V C Morris Gift Shop in 1949 and the Solomon R Guggenheim Museum from 1956, where the ramp formed the gallery walkway.

The V C Morris Gift Shop, acknowledged as one of the finest examples of American architecture of the twentieth century, illustrates how well Wright was able to take an ordinary building-type, a retail shop, and transform it into an architectural wonder. Outside the wall of narrow bricks, accentuating the horizontal elements of the build-ing, is broken by a Romanesque arch edged with four con-centric bands of bricks. Two rows of lights – one horizontal row of lighted glass bricks, the other a vertical band of small rectangular lights – lead to the archway entrance and inside, wherein lies the circular ramp. The customer travels up the ramp viewing the merchandise in glass enclosures and through circular openings.

In 1952 Wright again used the device of the ramp in his design for a small shopping center, the Anderton Court Shops at North Rodeo Drive in Beverly Hills. For this pro-ject Wright adopted a vertical form where four levels of shops and offices are linked together by the ramp. To emphasize this feature, the ramp winds around a mast, the stylized design of which looks to some like a sci-fi tower, to others like a single ear of wheat.

The Guggenheim Museum is often considered to be the climax of Wright's career, as it combined all the structural and spatial principles employed in *Fallingwater* with the roof-lit containment of the Johnson's Wax Building. How-ever, a project that was being designed and constructed at the time of his death in 1959, the Marin County Civic Center, can be seen as Wright's last statement on a scheme he had been developing since the 1930s.

In 1934 Wright designed a theoretical city – Broadacre City – in which he attempted to show the development of a large area of the United States when the once-prosperous nation re-emerged from the Depression. Not only would Broadacre City be the result of the new trend toward home-ownership, it would be shaped by the automobile, radio, telephones, and above all, by standardized machine-pro-duced materials. This ideal of the city is evident in the Marin County project, but in addition to being a horizontal city with internal road systems, the civic center is also an expression of Wright's view that in a democracy, it is the individual and his actions that are important. And so, in-side the complex there are public atria, auditoria, and libraries, there for the citizen to use and enjoy. The civic center remains, however, just a fragment of a dream city, a city for a universal middle-class society.

Gregor Affleck Residence,
1940
Bloomfield Hills, MI
Photo, © Balthazar Korab

Melvyn Maxwell Smith
Residence, 1946
Bloomfield Hills, MI
Photo, © Balthazar Korab

90

Mrs Clinton Walker
Residence, 1948
Carmel, CA
Photo, © Balthazar Korab

Unitarian Church, 1947
Bloomfield Hills, MI
Photo, © Balthazar Korab

Unitarian Church
Interior
Photo, © Balthazar Korab

Howard Anthony Residence,
1949
Benton Harbor, MI
Photo, © *Balthazar Korab*

Howard Anthony Residence
Interior
Photo, © Balthazar Korab

David Wright Residence, 1950
Phoenix, AZ
Photo, © *Pedro E. Guerrero*

David Wright Residence
Interior
Photo, © Pedro E. Guerrero

Top: Price Company Tower,
1952
Bartlesville, OK
Signed tile
*Photo, courtesy of Phillips
Petroleum*

Above: Price Tower
Detail of copper parapet
*Photo, courtesy of Phillips
Petroleum*

Opposite: Price Tower
Photo, © Balthazar Korab

Beth Shalom Synagogue, 1954
Elkins Park, PA
Photo, © Balthazar Korab

Kalita Humphreys Theater,
1955
Dallas, TX
Photo, © Balthazar Korab

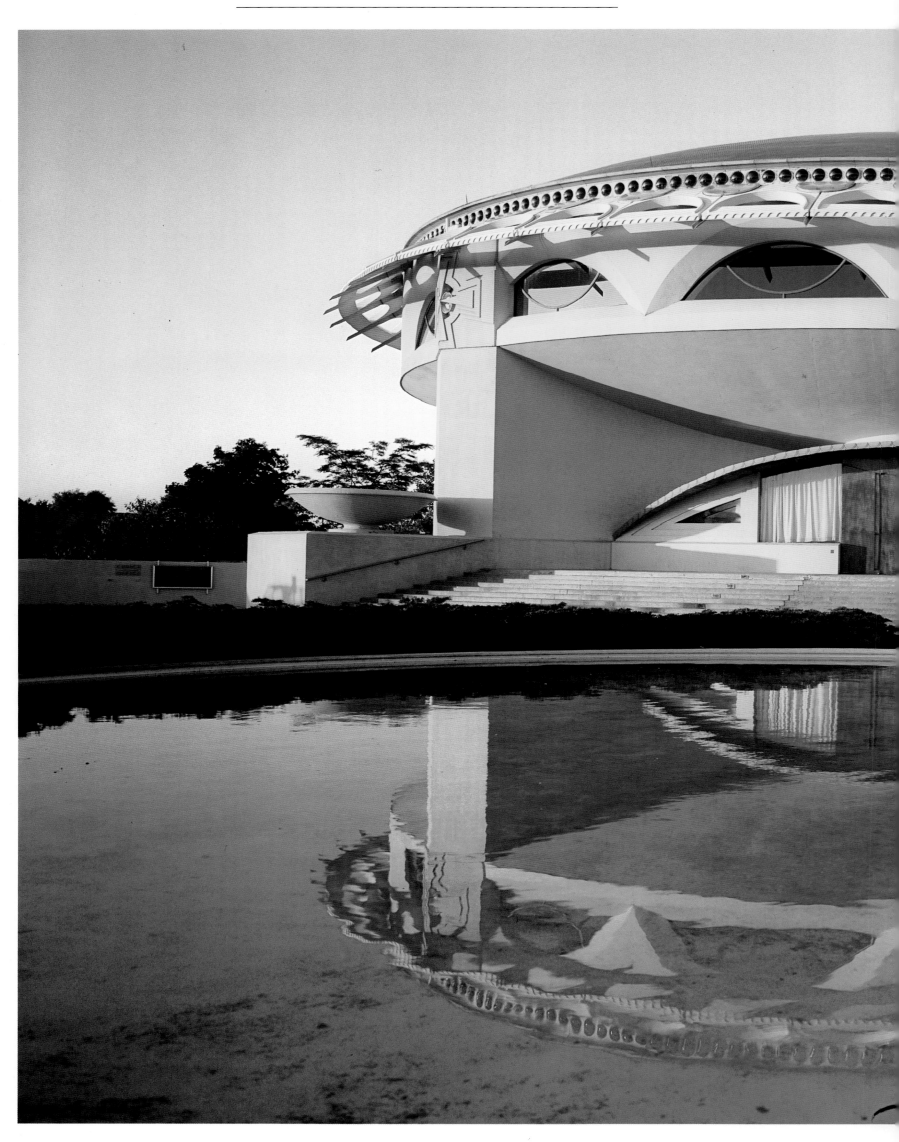

Annunciation Greek Orthodox
Church, 1956
Wauwatosa, WI
Photo, © Balthazar Korab

Annunciation Greek Orthodox
Church
Photo, © *Balthazar Korab*

Annunciation Greek Orthodox
Church
Photo, © Balthazar Korab

Above: Solomon R
Guggenheim Museum, 1956
New York, NY
Interior
Photo, © Balthazar Korab

Opposite: Solomon R
Guggenheim Museum
Photo, © Balthazar Korab

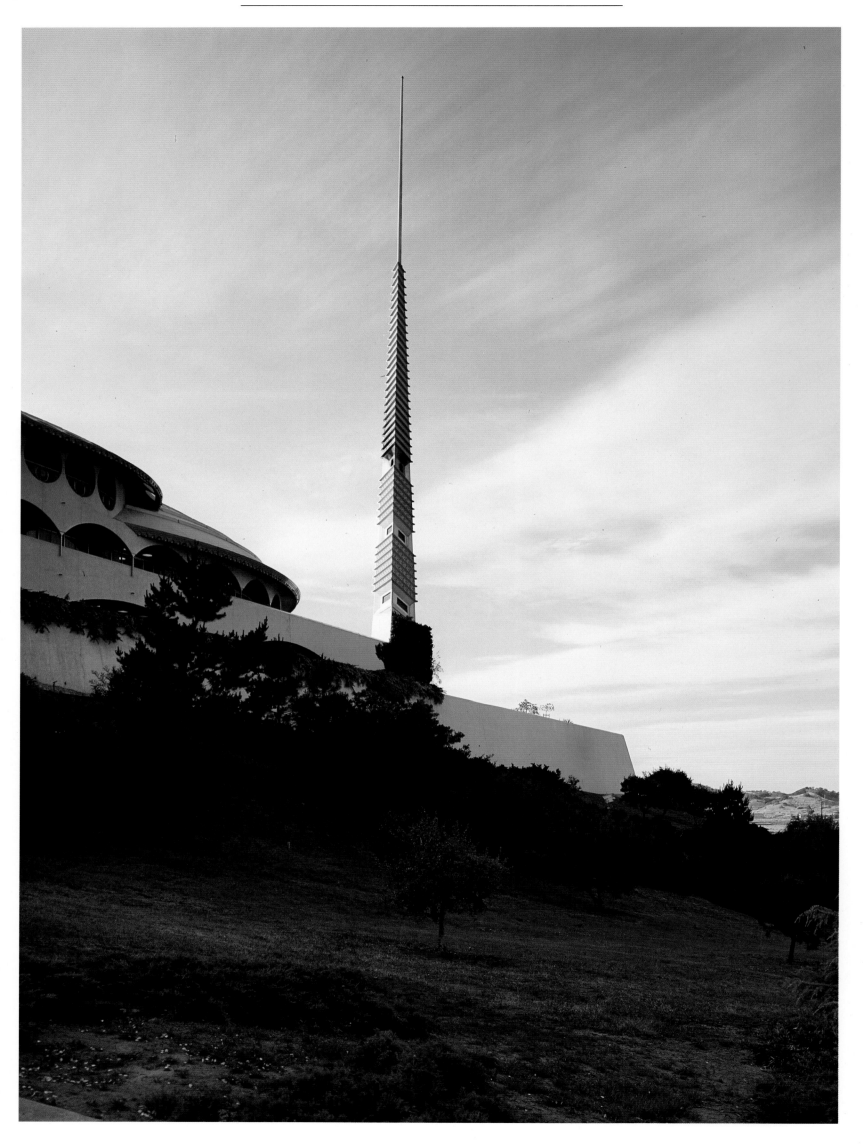

Top: Marin County Civic
Center, Administration
Building and Hall of Justice,
1957
San Raphael, CA
Photo, UPI/Bettmann

Right: Marin County Civic
Center
Detail of Balcony
Photo, © Balthazar Korab

Opposite: Marin County Civic
Center
Photo, © Balthazar Korab

Above: Arizona State
University, Grady Gammage
Auditorium, 1959
Temple, AZ
Photo, UPI/Bettmann

Opposite: Grady Gammage
Auditorium
Photo, © Balthazar Korab

INDEX

Figures in *italics* refer to illustrations

Adler and Sullivan 7, 8-9, 21
Adler, Dankmar 8
Affleck Residence 89
All Souls' Church 7, 21
Annunciation Greek Orthodox Church *102-5*
Arizona Biltmore 64-5
Arizona State University, Auditorium 110-111
Auditorium Building, Chicago 8

Barnsdall Residence *see* Hollyhock House
Beachy House 11
Beth Shalom Synagogue *100*
Blossom House 9, 21, *23*
Bock, Francis 22
Bradley, Harley 11

California Bungalow style 11
Cheney, Mrs Edwin 14
Cochrane, JL 21
Colonial style 21
Connover, Allen D 6, 7
Dana Residence 11, *40-41*
Dana, Susan Lawrence 12
Davenport House 11

Ennis Residence *14, 54, 58*

Fallingwater *15, 17, 68-9*
Florida Southern College 86-7
Francisco Terrace Apartments *36*
Fricke Residence 11, *34-5*
Furness, Frank 8

Gale, Thomas 9
    Walter 9, 21
Gale (Thomas) House 9
Gale (Walter) House 9, 21
Golden Gate, The 21
Griffin, Walter Burley 14
Guerrero, Pedro 17
Guggenheim Museum *18-19, 106-7*

Hanna Residence *see* Honeycomb House
Harem, The *see* Thomas Residence
Heller House 22
Heurtley Residence *43*
Hickox, Warren 11
Hillside Home School 21
Holcomb, Permilia 6
Hollyhock House *58*
Holst, Hermann Von 14
Honeycomb House *74-5*
Howard Anthony Residence *94-5*
Humphreys Theater *101*

Imperial Hotel, Tokyo *56-7*
Inland Architect and News Record 21

Jenney, William Le Baron 8
Johnson Residence *see* Wingspread
Johnson Wax Company Administration Building 15, *70-71*

Kauffmann, Edgar J Sr., House *see* Fallingwater

Larkin Company Administration Building 12, *12-13*, 15, 17
Lloyd-Jones, Anna 6
    Jane *7*, 21
    Neil 21
    Rev Jenkin 7

Mahoney, Marion 14
Marin County Civic Center *108-9*
Martin Residence 11, 15, *43*
May Residence *4-5, 48-53*
Mission House style 11
Moore, Nathan 9, 22
Moore Residence 22, *37*

Neidecken, George 51

Oak Park House *1*, 9, *11-12*, 20, *24-31, 33*

Pfeiffer Chapel *84*
Price Tower *98-9*

Rayward-Shepherd House *15*
Robie Residence *2, 38, 46-7*
Roloson Houses 22
Roloson, Robert W 22

Shaw, Norman 7
'Shingle style' 7, 21
Silsbee, Joseph Lyman 7, 21
Stewart House 14
Storer Residence *59*
Sturges Residence *66*
Sullivan, Louis 7-8, *8*, 22

Taliesin 14, *16-17, 60-63, 76-83*
Thomas House 11, *33*
Tobin, Catherine 7, 9
Transportation Building, Chicago *8*, 21, 22

Unitarian Chapel 21
Unitarian Church *92*
Unity Temple *44-5*

Walker Residence *91*
Whistler, J McN 8
Willit House 11
Wingspread *72-3*
Winslow Residence 21, *32*
Winslow, William H 9, 21, 22
Wright, Frank Lloyd 6, *7*, 9

Ausgefuerte Bauten und Entwerfe von Frank Lloyd Wright 11
autobiography 6, 9, 14, 17
'Bootlegged' houses 9
California 14
Chicago 7-14
construction techniques *18*
education 6, 9
function and form 6, 7, 9, 11, 15, 17, 21, 22
furnishings 11, 13-14
Hull House Lecture 9
Japanese influence 8, 22
Los Angeles 14
Prairie Houses 9-12, 14, 21, 22
pre-Columbian influence 8, 14
Small House with Lots of Room In It, A 11
travel to Europe 14
use of concrete 14
Usonian Houses 15, 17-18
Wright, Lloyd 7, 14
Wright (David) Residence *96-7*
Wright, William Russel Cary 6

ACKNOWLEDGMENTS

The publisher would like to thank Ron Callow of Design 23, who designed this book, Elizabeth Montgomery, the picture researcher, and the following individuals and agencies for supplying the illustrations to the introduction:

Ann Abernathy, courtesy of the Frank Lloyd Wright Home and Studio Foundation: page 1
Bettmann Archive: page 8
Buffalo and Erie County Historical Society: pages 12, 13
© Robert Frerck/Odyssey Productions: pages 2-3
© Pedro E. Guerrero: pages 15 (middle), 16, 17, 18 (top)
Peter Johnson, courtesy of the Frank Lloyd Wright Home and Studio Foundation: page 10
© Balthazar Korab: page 11, 15 (bottom)
Steelcase, Inc.: pages 4-5
© Ezra Stoller/Esto: pages 14, 19
UPI/Bettmann Newsphotos: page 18 (bottom)
Frank Lloyd Wright Home and Studio Foundation: pages 7, 9